D1360997

CLASSIC
StoryTellers

RAY BRADBURY

Mitchell Lane
PUBLISHERS

P.O. Box 196
Hockessin, Delaware 19707

Titles in the Series

C L A S S I C
StoryTellers

RAY BRADBURY

Michèle Griskey

s StoryTellers
ry StoryTellers
StoryTellers
Story Tellers
Story Tellers
Story Tellers
Story Tellers
Story T

Printing   1   2   3   4   5   6   7   8   9

Library of Congress Cataloging-in-Publication Data
Griskey, Michèle.
    Ray Bradbury / by Michèle Griskey.
        p. cm.—(Classic storytellers)
    Includes bibliographical references and index.
    ISBN 1-58415-455-1 (lib. bdg.)
1. Bradbury, Ray, 1920—Juvenile literature. 2. Authors, American—20th century—Biography—Juvenile literature. 3. Science fiction—Authorship—Juvenile literature. 4. Fantasy fiction—Authorship—Juvenile literature. I. Title. II. Series.
    PS3503.R167z686 2006
    813'.54—dc22

                                     2005027984
ISBN-10: 1-58415-455-1   ISBN-13: 978-158415-4556

ABOUT THE AUTHOR: Michèle Griskey has a BA in writing and an MA in English, with concentrations in literature and creative writing. She teaches writing, research, and philosophy for the University of Phoenix Online. She has written several biographies for Mitchell Lane Publishers, including *Harriet Beecher Stowe* and *Beverly Cleary*. As a child, she loved to watch the night sky and often wondered what it would be like to travel to other worlds. Michèle also writes fiction for middle grade and teen readers and lives on an island in Washington's Puget Sound with her family.

Contents

RAY BRADBURY

Michèle Griskey

*For Your Information

StoryTellers StoryTellers StoryTellers StoryTellers StoryTellers StoryTellers StoryTellers StoryTellers

A geodesic sphere over 165 feet in diameter welcomes visitors to Epcot Center at Walt Disney World in Florida. Inside the sphere is the ride Spaceship Earth, *which science fiction master Ray Bradbury helped design.*

Chapter 1

A LIFE OF IMAGINATION

Fireworks exploded in the sky over the Walt Disney World Resort in Orlando, Florida. A sixty-two year old man stood watching with tears in his eyes. It was the opening celebration of Disney's Epcot Center. The man was science fiction writer Ray Bradbury, and he was thinking about his past.

Bradbury had been invited to Florida because he had helped design the *Spaceship Earth* exhibit. The outside of the exhibit is an enormous geodesic sphere made of over eleven thousand triangular panels. It measures over 165 feet in diameter and took two years and two months to build. *Spaceship Earth* tells the story of communication through time, starting with the days of primitive cave drawings and taking the rider past other high points in history, such as the invention of the printing press and the telephone, and speculation on how humans would communicate in the future.

Although he had designed the exhibit to include technological marvels, there were some types of technology Bradbury avoided in his life. Instead of boarding an airplane for the eight-hour flight, he had traveled to Florida all the way from California by railroad, limousine, and taxi. It had taken days to arrive. Bradbury didn't drive, and up to that point, he had been afraid to fly.

As he gazed at the Epcot exhibit, Bradbury was thinking about what the future could be like.[1] He may also have been remembering times before Disney World (which opened in 1971) or even California's Disneyland (which opened in 1955), when he had attended world's fairs as a child. He had been dazzled by the exhibits showing the wonders of the future. He remembered how he wanted to one day be a part of designing something that made others marvel about what life in the future could be like. He had grown up in the 1920s and 1930s, when space travel was a fantasy rather than reality. Forty years later, he interviewed the *Apollo 1* astronauts as they prepared for their journey to the moon.

He had met and snapped pictures of movie stars in Hollywood. More than anything, he had wanted others to take notice of him, to see him as someone important.

He may have remembered meeting Walt Disney and hearing Disney's dream for creating a permanent world's fair as a theme park. Bradbury was now standing in Disney's dream—and living his own.

Bradbury stood in front of something he had once only imagined. So much in his life began with just that—imagination. While the massive *Spaceship Earth* was an awe-inspiring accomplishment, his creativity shone brightest in the words that he wrote, the stories that sprang from his mind: stories about journeys to other planets; stories about his past, growing up in a small Midwestern town and enjoying the thrill of a carnival or the mystery of his favorite holiday, Halloween. A writer, a spokesman, a designer, and a visionary—many of the things that Bradbury had dreamed about had come true.

Yet Bradbury's career was far from over. He had more work to do and more life to experience. In fact, he rode an airplane for the first time on the way home.

FYInfo

Carnivals

The origin of the word *carnival* comes from the word *carnevale,* which means "to put away the meat." This reflected the European festivals that took place right before the Catholic season of Lent. Since people were not supposed to eat meat during Lent, the days before this period were a time when people dressed up and celebrated. These carnival celebrations are still held in many parts of the world.

Carnivals took on different meanings in the United States. In places like New Orleans, the carnival celebrations are based on the European tradition, but "carnival" also became an offshoot of circus sideshows. Instead of having one performance (like a small circus), a carnival was a collection of shorter shows with tents containing bizarre or unusual people or objects. They also included amusement rides and attractions such as carousels and fun houses. With the arrival of the railroad, these shows became very popular in the late nineteenth century and continued in popularity in the twentieth century. The carnivals would move from town to town by train and set up tents and rides in open spaces.

Carnivals often had performers who would do unusual or dangerous acts, such as individuals who would swallow swords or breathe fire; contortionists who would bend themselves into pretzel shapes; and magicians who would dazzle the crowds with their tricks.

A Contortionist

Other attractions would include a collection of "freaks," which in modern society would be considered cruel. People with conditions that made them look different were put on display—such as the "fat lady" (an obese woman) or the "lizard boy" (a boy with a skin problem). Often these people were shunned by regular society, and the carnivals offered them a way to make a living. Carnivals provided an element of excitement, mystery, and magic to people living in the United States and in other parts of the world.

The rise of permanent theme parks such as Disneyland, Six Flags, and others caused the popularity of carnivals to diminish. Carnivals still exist, traveling from town to town, often to help organizations such as fire departments raise money. The focus has turned more on the rides, games, and food rather than performers.

A crystal radio, like the one Ray Bradbury's grandfather built in 1922, is the simplest kind of radio. It uses a crystal diode to extract the audio signal from the radio signal for the listener to hear with the headphones. Crystal radios do not require electricity or batteries.

Chapter 2

FILMS, BOOKS, AND COMIC STRIPS

On August 22, 1920, Rae Douglas Bradbury was born in Waukegan, Illinois, which is on the shores of Lake Michigan. *Rae* would later become *Ray,* when a schoolteacher suggested to his parents that *Ray* looked more like a boy's name. His parents, Esther and Leonard Bradbury, had been married in 1914. Two years later, they became the parents of twin boys— Leonard Jr. (or "Skip," as he was called) and Samuel. Tragically, Samuel died in the Spanish influenza epidemic in 1918. Later, when Ray was six, his sister Elizabeth was born. She also died, in 1928, after being ill. Understandably, Esther Bradbury became very protective of her two surviving sons.

Ray spent his early years in Waukegan, which would later serve as the small-town Midwestern setting in a number of his stories. As he grew, inventions and popular culture became some of the biggest influences on him. In 1922, his grandfather built a crystal radio. At that time, radios were the primary way people connected with the rest of the world. It was through radio that Ray heard music, dramatic shows, and news. Esther Bradbury liked to take her youngest son to the movie theater. She loved films and passed her passion on to Ray. He remembered seeing the silent film *The Hunchback of Notre Dame* with his mother when he was three. He saw *Phantom of the Opera* a few years later. Both films left a strong impression on him. At the age of nine, Ray discovered the comic strip *Buck Rogers in the 25th Century*. He became a fan of the futuristic hero, who used ray guns to do battle with intergalactic bad guys. "When Buck Rogers came along, instantly, within the very first strip I just went absolutely crazy. I'd just started with the most *amazing* thing I'd ever seen; could barely *wait* through each day. That's the way I lived. I lived hysterically, waiting for that hour every afternoon when Buck Rogers came into the house."[1]

Ray also began to read books and spent a great deal of time at the Carnegie Library, the public library near his home. There he developed his love for reading with popular literature of the time, like the *Oz* series by L. Frank Baum (which would later be made into the classic movie *The Wizard of Oz*), and the Nancy Drew mysteries (though Ray didn't want others to know he read books for girls). Through his uncle, Bion Bradbury, Ray also discovered the literature of Edgar Rice Burroughs, who wrote the Tarzan books and a series of novels that take place on Mars. These books inspired Ray to use the same setting for his book about Mars, *The Martian Chronicles*. In addition to books and comic strips, he also discovered science fiction in magazines such as *Amazing Stories Quarterly*. He found the pictures and stories fascinating.

Another influence on young Ray was his aunt Nevada, whom everyone called Neva. Only ten years older than Ray, she introduced him to literature and art. When Ray was five, she gave him a book of fairy tales called *Once Upon a Time*, which introduced the world of fantasy to him. In the years to come, Neva's exploration of the artistic world opened up a number of possibilities for her nephew that were not available in his everyday life. In an interview in 1964,

Bradbury explained, "My aunt Neva helped bring me up in a world of let's-pretend, in a world of masks and puppets that she made, in a world of stages and acting, in a world of special Christmases and Halloweens."[2]

He also discovered magic. In 1928, Blackstone the Magician visited Waukegan. Ray went to all of his shows and took notes on the tricks he saw. On a return visit, Blackstone invited Ray on stage as an assistant for one of his illusions. Ray wanted to become a magician, too, and worked diligently to learn new tricks. He began performing magic shows for his family.

Another experience that meant a great deal to Ray was seeing a carnival performance of Mr. Electrico, who was part of the Dill Brothers Combined Shows. Dill Brothers was visiting Waukegan on Labor Day Weekend in 1932. At that time carnivals provided thrilling entertainment, with acts of daring and illusion. Mr. Electrico was no exception. This magician would sit in a charged electric chair. When a switch was flipped on, Mr. Electrico came to life. Strapped in the chair, jolts of electricity zapped through his body. Charged with the electrical currents, Mr. Electrico would then hold a sword over the children in the audience. The electricity in the sword caused the children's hair to stand up. This was an amazing spectacle for young Ray. Mr. Electrico selected Ray from the crowd. He tapped his brow with the sword and said, "Live forever."

"I decided it was the greatest idea I had ever heard," Ray later said of the magician's spell.[3]

That Labor Day weekend was a time of transition for Ray. He had just lost an uncle, and on the day after experiencing Mr. Electrico's performance, he was riding back with his family from his uncle's funeral. Ray made his dad stop the car near the carnival tents and asked to be let out. He ran down the hill so that he could talk to Mr. Electrico again. He spent time visiting the magician and meeting the other performers in the carnival. Later Ray would write, "What was I doing? I was running away from death, running towards life."[4]

Obviously, he couldn't actually live forever, but the words of the magician inspired the young boy to create a kind of immortality through language. Soon after this experience, Ray began to write.

When the United States was struggling through the Great Depression, the Bradbury family, like millions of other Americans, faced economic hardships. In 1926, they had moved to Tucson, Arizona, but they'd returned to Waukegan in 1927 after Ray's father couldn't find work. From 1927 to 1932, the Bradbury family stayed in Waukegan until Mr. Bradbury decided again to move to Tucson to gain any kind of employment he could find.

In Tucson, Ray made new friends and had his first taste of acting in the school Christmas play, *A Wooden Shoe Christmas.* He enjoyed being on stage and added acting to the things he wanted to do. KGAR, the radio station near where Ray lived, performed the show *Chandu the Magician,* a favorite radio program of Ray's. He decided that he wanted to work there. After being a pest at the station and running errands for the staff, Ray was invited to go on the air. He worked with other children by providing voices and sound effects. He read Sunday comics on the air in exchange for free movie tickets.

In addition to magic and radio, Ray worked on becoming a writer. For Christmas in 1932, he got his first typewriter, which was made for children but worked like a real one. Ray used it to write a sequel to Edgar Rice Burroughs's Martian novels, scripts for *Buck Rogers,* and letters to his family back home. The stay in Tucson would not be long, however. The Bradbury family moved back to Waukegan in 1933.

Back in Waukegan, Ray had the opportunity to go to the Century of Progress World's Fair in Chicago. These fairs had become popular during the 1800s and were held every few years. Various cities around the world hosted them. They featured displays on ideas and concepts of the future. For example, people at the fair could visit what a house of the future would look like. The fair also had exhibits that featured Asian gardens or simulated streets in Paris. Ray found the futuristic architecture displays amazing and was inspired to create his own world's fair out of cardboard. Many years later, his love of architecture would pay off when he would be asked to consult on some buildings of the future. For the young Ray, it became another interesting imaginative possibility for him to explore.

In 1934, after being laid off from the utility company where he worked, Ray's father decided to move his family to Los Angeles, where Ray's uncle and aunt had moved. In his new hometown, Ray sought out movie studios and theaters. He said, "I was madly in love with Hollywood. We lived about four blocks from the Uptown Theater, which was the flagship theater for MGM and Fox. I learned how to sneak in. There were previews almost every week."[5]

Dashing down streets on his roller skates, Ray also went in search of Hollywood celebrities. He wasn't shy, so he had no reservations about asking stars for their autographs, and sometimes, when his father would let him borrow the camera, he would get pictures of himself with some big Hollywood celebrities. Living in Los Angeles whetted Ray's desire to become a writer and an actor.

One day while skating in front of the Figueroa Street Playhouse, Ray met comedian George Burns. Burns had a radio show with his wife, Gracie Allen, who was also a talented comedian. Ray talked Burns into letting him and a friend sit through rehearsals of the show. Inspired, Ray began to write scripts for the Burns and Allen Show. George Burns would read the scripts and say nice things to Ray, but he didn't use anything in the show. In 1936, Burns and Allen used one of Ray's jokes on the air, which, of course, thrilled the young writer.

Though Ray loved the glamour of Hollywood, he also experienced something frightening. In 1935, while visiting a high school friend, Eddie Barrera, he and Eddie heard a crash. They ran outside to find that a horrible automobile accident had just occurred. A car had hit a telephone pole and three people were dead. A fourth, a woman, looked up at Ray for a moment before she died, too. This terrifying experience impacted Ray greatly. As a result, he never learned how to drive a car.

In high school, Ray took writing classes to help develop his skills. Though he was outwardly confident about his writing, he didn't have great social skills with some of the other students. He was shy around girls and bullied by some of the boys. Nevertheless, he kept the confidence that he would be a great writer someday. He had his first publishing success in 1936 when his poem "In Memory to Will Rogers" was printed in the *Waukegan News-Sun*. The poem commemorated the life and tragic death of Will Rogers. The popular film star and writer had died in an airplane crash in 1935. In 1937, when Ray was a junior in high school, he wrote and directed the school talent show called *Roman Review*.

In school he enrolled in a poetry class and a short story class. He began developing a consistent schedule by writing every day; eventually he would be writing about one short story a week, and this was a schedule he would keep long after high school. These early stories were inspired mostly by what Ray read, and he had yet to find

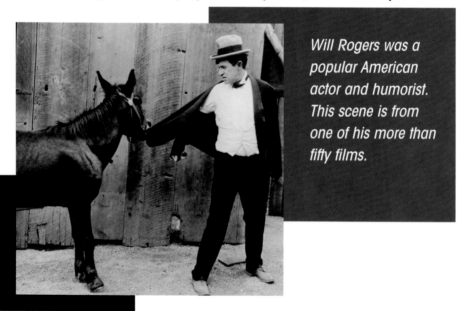

Will Rogers was a popular American actor and humorist. This scene is from one of his more than fifty films.

his unique writer's voice. Outside of school, he joined the Los Angeles chapter of the Science Fiction Society, where he met other fans and writers of science fiction. Many of these people—including future science fiction masters Robert Heinlein, Forrest J. Ackerman (the founder of the society), and Leigh Brackett—would encourage Ray as he followed his dream to become a great writer. In 1938, his short story "Hollerbochen's Dilemma" was published in the society's fanzine *Imagination!*

In 1938 Ray Bradbury graduated from Los Angeles High School and took a job selling newspapers—*The Herald Express*—on a street corner in the city. He worked in the afternoon and wrote in the morning. He enjoyed his work because he was able to spend time with people, and though he didn't earn a great deal of money, he earned enough to meet his modest expenses.

Ray decided not to go to college. Instead, he continued to educate himself by visiting the library several times a week and reading regularly. He also continued to seek the advice of the writers in the Science Fiction Society.

In June of 1939, Ray had the opportunity to go the New York City to attend the first World Science Fiction Convention. This was a significant time for the science fiction genre because it marked the first time a group of fans would get together and share their enthusiasm. Ray loved being a part of the movement and felt even more determined to become a great writer. He also visited the World's Fair, which was being held in Queens, New York, that year. As with the World's Fair of 1933, Ray loved seeing the exhibits, which included a planetarium and an early television set.

In 1940, Ray had his first commercial success—a short story published in a Hollywood literary magazine called *Script*. He continued to sell stories to more magazines, but in the following year, world events would interfere with his writing career in a significant way.

On December 7, 1941, the Japanese attacked Pearl Harbor, and the United States entered World War II. Since Ray was old enough to go to war, he worried that he would be drafted and sent overseas to fight. He was terrified of dying in the war or being bullied by the other soldiers. In 1942, when he reported for his physical, he was excused by the draft board because of his poor eyesight and was sent home. Ray wanted to contribute to the war effort, however, so he wrote promotional material for the American Red Cross.

During this year Ray had a breakthrough in his writing. He wrote a story based on something from his past. "The Lake" became what he considered his "first great story."[6] It was based on a memory he had of a young girl who drowned in Lake Michigan. The story was the first to showcase Bradbury's unique voice and writing style, and was the first of many great stories to come.

Bradbury continued his schedule of writing one story a week, and by 1944 he had sold twenty-two stories. In 1945, writer and publisher August Derleth showed interest in his work and offered to help him put together a collection of his stories. This would become Bradbury's first book, *Dark Carnival.* Also, Bradbury started submitting stories to literary magazines. Up until this point, his work was exclusively in "pulp" science fiction and fantasy magazines. "Pulp" is writing considered to be of lesser quality than literary fiction. It was printed in magazines made of cheap wood pulp paper. Often pulp stories focused on exciting or bizarre events to keep the readers interested. Jumping from the pulp magazines to the mainstream "glossy" magazines was no easy feat, because "pulp writers" were not considered as sophisticated or as polished as the mainstream magazine writers. Using the pseudonym William Elliot, Bradbury submitted stories to three mainstream magazines. Amazingly, all three were accepted for publication. Additionally, his story "The Big Black and White Game" was selected to be included in the anthology *The Best American Short Stories of the Year.*

Bradbury quit his job selling newspapers and began writing full-time. He was indeed becoming the great writer he had only dreamed about a few years before.

FYInfo

Buck Rogers in the 25th Century

Thirty years before NASA was founded, when the idea of space travel was still a dream, "Armageddon-2419 A.D.," by Philip Francis Nowlan, appeared in the August 1928 issue of *Amazing Stories*. This short story would provide a basis for the first science fiction comic strip. *Buck Rogers in the 25th Century,* which debuted in U.S. newspapers in 1929, was written by Nowlan and illustrated by Richard Calkins. The comic strip told the story of Buck Rogers and his adventures on an Earth of the future.

The story begins with Buck Rogers as a 20th-century mine surveyor who becomes trapped in a mine. A radioactive gas puts Rogers in a state of suspended animation for 500 years. In other words, he is kept alive, but he doesn't age. When he awakens in the 25th century, the world is in violent chaos, but it also has a mind-boggling supply of hi-tech marvels.

Buck becomes a hero as he works with the characters Wilma Deering and Dr. Huer to defeat the "bad guys" the Mongols, Killer Kane, and Ardala. Peppering the classic good-versus-evil storyline are the amazing gadgets Rogers uses, including ray guns and rocket ships. These comic strip adventures found a great following. It was published in 400 newspapers and translated into 18 languages. In 1932

A Buck Rogers Painting
by Anton Brzezinski

a radio show of Buck Rogers began to air, which increased the story's popularity. Buck Rogers generated a great deal of merchandise, including toys—like ray guns—and clothing. In 1934 a department store used an actor dressed as Buck Rogers instead of their usual Santa Claus for the holiday season.

The original comic strip, which ran for 38 years, eventually led to Buck Rogers television shows, movies, and, more recently, role-playing and computer games. The comic strip also inspired other science fiction series such as *Flash Gordon.* With his stories, Nowlan started a popular movement for young people to speculate on what the future would be like and what kinds of adventures they would find. It also brought the dream of space travel closer to reality.

A 1952 publicity photo of Ray Bradbury. His career was just starting to take off after the publication of The Martian Chronicles and The Illustrated Man.

Chapter 3

THE JOURNEY TO SUCCESS

A young man walking through Fowler Brothers Bookstore in Los Angeles caught an employee's eye. Marguerite McClure had been told to watch for shoplifters, and this young man looked suspicious—he was wearing a trench coat on a warm day. After approaching the man, Marguerite soon learned that she was not speaking to a criminal but instead to a writer who was beginning to make a name for himself—Ray Bradbury. Marguerite and Ray began to talk and found that they enjoyed each other's company. Soon they were dating each other, and then were very much in love. Ray and Maggie (as she was called) eventually got engaged. Ray liked Maggie because she knew a great deal about literature and culture. Maggie liked Ray because of his enthusiasm for his writing and life. During this time, Ray had some big jumps in his career. In 1947, *Dark Carnival* was published. In addition, his story "Homecoming" had been selected for the anthology *The O. Henry Prize Stories of 1947*.

Ray and Maggie were married that year on September 27, and they rented a little apartment near

Venice Beach, California. Ray was making money as a writer, but he didn't earn very much. Though it was uncharacteristic for the era, Maggie was the primary wage earner. She had a job as a secretary, while Ray stayed home and wrote. Over the following years Ray continued to write and publish stories, but in 1949, Maggie became pregnant and, characteristic for the times, would have to leave her job. Ray needed to do something bigger. On the advice of a friend, he decided to go to New York City and meet some editors. Since he didn't have a great deal of money, he traveled by bus and stayed at the YMCA when he arrived. Most of the publishers he met were not interested in a collection of short stories, but he finally found an editor who was. Walter Bradbury (not related to Ray) of Doubleday told Ray he would like to see a collection of his stories about Mars. He advanced him some money for the project, and Ray returned to Los Angeles. He'd have to complete the book in three months.

Ray brought together a series of stories he had about Mars and linked these to ideas he had about the Old West and the Western expansion on Earth. A lot more is known about Mars now than was known in the 1950s; even so, Ray decided to use an older, more romantic version of Mars from the nineteenth and early twentieth centuries. He portrayed Martians who created beautiful cities, used channels for irrigation, and had the ability to foresee the future. He wrote about Mars with a breathable atmosphere, which made it intriguing for explorers from Earth. In addition, the book dealt with important social issues such as racism and nuclear warfare. The collection would become his celebrated work, *The Martian Chronicles*.

Ray and Maggie became the proud parents of Susan Marguerite on November 5, 1949. Though their financial situation was improving some, the Bradbury family of three still struggled.

The following year *The Martian Chronicles* was published. On a trip to New York in May, Ray stopped off in Chicago to meet a fan. On the steps of the Art Institute of Chicago, a small group of people stood waiting for him to sign their brand-new copies of *The Martian*

Chronicles. Bradbury said, "I was suddenly being accepted and loved and read, and here were fourteen strangers showing up to congratulate me on this change in my life."[1] He had broken through; he now had a real following as a writer.

Once Bradbury's writing career had taken off, he started lecturing about writing at a number of universities. Like his unplanned writing, Bradbury preferred a spontaneous speaking style, and audiences enjoyed his honesty and passion. In 1951 he published *The Illustrated Man,* which also became very popular. That year, he and Maggie welcomed another daughter, Ramona. Ray also worked on *It Came From Outer Space,* a film that reflected the popularity of science fiction and the idea of extraterrestrials at that time. Soon after, his short story collection *The Golden Apples of the Sun* was published and achieved critical acclaim.

While positive things were happening for Bradbury, a new fear was gripping the country. It was the fear of a political system very different from the democratic government and private industry established in the United States: a fear of communism. In 1950, Joseph McCarthy, a Republican senator, publicly claimed that there were communists in the State Department. The statement, picked up by the press, started an enormous uproar. Many people were blacklisted. Accused of being communists, they where kept out of the workforce and shunned by many. These accusations were based on little evidence, and soon there was a panic throughout the nation that communists were everywhere and threatening to take over the country.

This volatile political climate reminded Bradbury of library burnings that had taken place in various times in history. He remembered the newsreels showing Nazis burning books during World War II. These memories mingled together in the back of his mind, and a story idea developed. He explained, "Since I am a library person and I've grown up in libraries and been educated by them and never made it to college, the library, to me, is central to my life."[2]

Joseph McCarthy was a Republican senator from 1947 to 1957. During his time in office, he claimed that people in the U.S. government were involved in communist activities. Though most of his claims could not be proven, McCarthy contributed to the panic felt during the Cold War era in the United States.

Interestingly, in a library was where his new book came together. While browsing in the library at UCLA, he discovered a typing room for college students. In the days before computers, students could use typewriters that were equipped with a timer. The cost was ten cents for every half hour. It was in this library typewriting room that Bradbury began crafting his new novel, a story inspired by the horrors of book burning and censorship. It was the story of Montag, a fireman of the future whose job was to burn books. Originally published as the story "The Fireman," it was later rewritten and published as the novel *Fahrenheit 451*. The title refers to the temperature needed to burn books. The novel would go on to become Bradbury's best-selling work.

Years later, in an interview in 1975, Bradbury talked about the connection between writing a book about an oppressive society and the fears developed during the McCarthy years in the United States. He said, "I wrote *Fahrenheit 451* to prevent book-burnings, not to induce that future into happening, or even to say that it was inevitable."[3] Though he wrote in response to the book burnings of the past, the book also seemed timely because of McCarthyism. Bradbury would say that the novel "was a direct attack on the kind of thought-destroying force [Joseph McCarthy] represented in the world."[4] Though other writers were being accused of being communists for writing controversial material, *Fahrenheit 451* and its author were left alone. Bradbury felt that he wasn't attacked because his novel was science fiction. Even though it reflected real events, it took place in an imaginary world of the future. It included details that seemed unimaginable in the 1950s. Interestingly, many of them actually came to exist: portable music (with headphones), room-sized television screens, and reality television are all part of the story.

Also in the 1950s, an exciting thing happened for Bradbury. John Huston, a movie director whom Bradbury admired greatly, asked Ray to come to Ireland with him to write a screenplay based on the novel *Moby Dick* by Herman Melville. Soon, the Bradbury family—Ray, Maggie, Susan, and Ramona (along with a nanny for the girls)—made their way to New York. They then took a ship to France and eventually to Ireland, where they stayed for six months. Ray found the time in Dublin very stressful. The task of turning the classic novel into a screenplay for a great director was a little more than nerve-wracking for this writer who was used to coming up with strange stories from his imagination. John Huston turned out to have a temper and liked to tease Ray. Since Ray was sensitive, he didn't respond well to this treatment. Despite these challenges, Bradbury managed to write the screenplay, and in 1956, it was made into a successful movie. The experience left a strong impression on the writer, and he used Ireland as a setting for some of his stories. Much later, in 1992, he published a book called *Green Shadows, White Whale* about his experience with John Huston in Ireland.

After returning to the United States, Bradbury turned down many offers to do more screenplays. He wanted to spend time with his family and devote his energy to his main passion—writing fiction. In July 1955, Bettina joined the other daughters in the Bradbury family. Ray's children's book *Switch On the Night* was published. The book is a story of a young boy who is afraid of the dark until he meets a girl named Dark who shows him that the dark isn't scary. Another book for older readers, *The October Country,* was also published.

During the 1950s, television grew in popularity. Bradbury began to write for *Alfred Hitchcock Presents*. Alfred Hitchcock, a popular director of suspense films, and Bradbury worked well together. Bradbury wrote several scripts for Hitchcock and enjoyed his work.

At this time Bradbury gathered a number of stories based on his memories of growing up in Illinois. He explained that while writing them, he found himself on "a rummage through a fabled attic or basement storehouse"[5] of his past. These stories turned into the book *Dandelion Wine,* which tells of twelve-year-old Douglas Spaulding and his adventures growing up in the Midwest during the 1920s.

In 1957, Bradbury had another opportunity to go to Europe to work on a screenplay. This one was based on his story "And the Rock

Alfred Hitchcock was a successful film director and producer who focused on horror and suspense. He made many films that became classics, including Vertigo, North by Northwest, The Birds, and Psycho. From 1955 to 1962, Hitchcock produced a popular television series called Alfred Hitchcock Presents.

Cried Out." The screenplay, though considered excellent, was never made into a movie. Unfortunately, Bradbury received more bad news when he returned home: his father had been sick. He had inflammation in the abdominal region. In the following months, Leo Bradbury suffered a stroke. He died in October 1957.

In August 1958, the final daughter, Alexandra, joined the Bradbury household. With four young girls, the Bradburys decided to find a bigger house. They moved to one in Cheviot Hills—where Ray Bradbury still lives. This house was bigger not only for the family but also for their enormous book collection. It also had basement space for Ray to set up his office. Ray and Maggie had come a long way from their tiny apartment in Venice Beach.

Bradbury continued to write scripts for television and other stories. He also wrote a novel, *Something Wicked This Way Comes,* which incorporated his love for carnivals. As with *Dandelion Wine,* this book was set in the Midwest. The idea for the book came about after Ray and Maggie went to a screening of a movie by dancer and director Gene Kelly. Bradbury decided that he wanted to work on a film with Kelly, so he went through his files to find a suitable story for a screenplay. In an interview in 1968, Ray said he wanted to write a book about boys and the adventures they go on where "they do all the great wild things boys relish and want to do in their heads and hope to do in the world."[6] He found one he'd written about two boys and a strange carnival, and turned this into an outline and script. Kelly thought the story was wonderful and offered to find funding for it in Europe so that it could be turned into a film. When no one funded the movie, the script was rewritten as a novel. *Something Wicked This Way Comes* was published in 1962.

Bradbury now had written many successful books. He had written for film and television as well. What would be next?

FYInfo

Mars

Mars is the fourth planet from the sun and a place where, some speculate, Earthlings may one day set up colonies to live. Since humans first gazed at the night sky, their imaginations have run wild. What if there *is* other intelligent life in the universe? With the discovery of planets, especially planets close to Earth, the idea that there could be other living beings nearby seemed plausible.

In the nineteenth century, Italian astronomer Giovanni Virginio Schiaparelli used the term *canale* to describe the long straight lines he saw on Mars. *Canale* means "channel," and the lines were considered a natural phenomenon. However, the word was mistranslated as "canal." Since canals have to be created by a life-form, people grew very excited about the possibility of life on Mars. From this misunderstanding, a myth was born.

Later Percival Lowell, a wealthy man who built an observatory in Arizona, expanded the theory that Mars had canals. He also observed lines on the surface of the planet and concluded that intelligent life must have made irrigation canals to get water from the poles to the dry middle region of the planet. Other observers doubted Lowell, but he developed quite a following. As

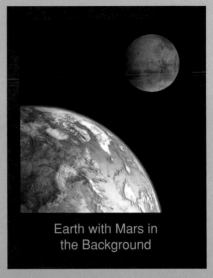

Earth with Mars in the Background

the twentieth century progressed, more and more evidence revealed that Mars probably couldn't sustain life as we know it. A thinner atmosphere, more extreme temperatures, and finally, in the 1960s, photographic evidence from the probe *Mariner IV* showed that the Martian canals were merely an optical illusion.

Other missions have shown similar details that *Mariner IV* showed, enforcing the belief that Mars is without life. In 2004, the NASA Mars Exploration Rovers *Spirit* and *Opportunity* landed on the Red Planet to explore its landscape. Though these robots have made many exciting discoveries, Martians have yet to be found.

As Ray Bradbury became more and more successful, he watched as science fiction became science fact. When NASA prepared astronauts to go to the moon, America looked to Bradbury as a symbol for the space age.

Chapter 4

THE MOON AND BEYOND

During the 1960s, Bradbury found himself in demand for new projects. First he was offered a job as a consultant for the U.S. Pavilion at the 1964 New York World's Fair. He designed a program on the history of the United States. The exhibit, called *American Journey,* used a moving platform, a film, and props. Creating this project was an exciting honor for a man who had enjoyed attending the World's Fairs in 1933 and 1939. Bradbury attended the fair with his family in 1964. In addition to the U.S. Pavilion, there was a replica of a nineteenth-century Bavarian village and an exhibit featuring an early computer.

In 1964, shopping for Christmas presents, Bradbury saw Walt Disney in a department store. Bradbury, who had long considered Disney a hero, introduced himself, and Disney invited him out to lunch. The men discovered that they had the same fascination for fairs, and Disney told Bradbury about his plans to make a permanent exhibition that would be like a world's fair. Later, in 1976, Bradbury was hired as a consultant for the Epcot Center,

Disney's vision for a world's fair. Bradbury designed the amusement ride *Spaceship Earth,* which would be built inside an enormous geodesic sphere. The ride opened in 1982 and remains the most popular attraction at Epcot.

In 1964, Bradbury had another collection of short stories published, *The Machineries of Joy.* In 1966, the film version of *Fahrenheit 451* was released. Later *The Illustrated Man* was also made into a film—but neither film did as well as the original books. These years brought about success for Bradbury, and he enjoyed time with his family, wife, and growing daughters. He was saddened, however, when his mother died in 1966.

The division between science fiction and science fact was becoming blurry during this time. The Soviet Union and the United States were involved in a race to begin the exploration of space. In 1957, the Soviet Union launched a satellite into orbit. In 1958, the United States created the National Aeronautics and Space Administration (NASA). Three years later, U.S. President John F. Kennedy addressed Congress with a declaration that surprised many people: "I believe this nation should commit itself to achieving the goal, before this decade is out, of landing a man on the moon and returning him safely to the earth."[1] This statement seemed next to impossible. The biggest achievement the U.S. had made by that time was Alan Shepard's suborbital flight. Going to the moon would require a great deal more work.

In an interview in 1990, Bradbury talked about the connection between the real world and science fiction: "How do you go to the Moon, huh? Science fiction, just forty years ago. Impossible! I had to put up with people saying to me, when I was thirty: 'We're never going to do that! Come on, don't be stupid. It's a silly thing to even think about. Why go to the moon? Why go to Mars?' Well, all of a sudden, just a few years ago, we solved the problem. So the science fictional dream became the Apollo missions."[2]

Alan B. Shepard Jr. tests his pressure suit as he prepares for launch. On May 5, 1961, he became the first American to fly into space. His Freedom 7 Mercury capsule flew a suborbital trajectory lasting 15 minutes and 22 seconds.

After Kennedy's declaration, the people in NASA's Apollo program worked diligently to achieve the president's vision. As more and more people became interested in the space race, Bradbury became a sort of unofficial connection between the world of the imaginary—the worlds he made up in his stories—and the real world.

In January 1967, Bradbury was invited to write a story about the *Apollo 1* crew. He went to Houston to meet the astronauts and tour the space center. Bradbury had a remarkable visit. He made friends with many of the astronauts, some of whom had been inspired by *The Martian Chronicles* to reach for space.

A few days later, after returning to Los Angeles and completing his article, Maggie came in and woke him from a nap. He stared at his television set and cried. The *Apollo 1* crew—Virgil "Gus" Grissom, Edward White, and Roger Chaffee—had been killed. During a test on the ground, the cockpit caught fire. Unable to escape, the three men died. Bradbury's article appeared in *Life* magazine almost a year after the tragedy.

Bradbury remained popular among astronauts. In 1971, the crew of *Apollo 15* became the first to use a moon rover. They christened a lunar crater "Dandelion" in honor of *Dandelion Wine.* Eight years later, Bradbury was the host for the television show *Infinite Horizons: Space Beyond Apollo,* which commemorated the 1969 landing of the *Apollo 11* crew on the moon. Though Bradbury wasn't an astronaut or a scientist—in fact he didn't even drive a car and refused to fly in an airplane for many years—he had captured the imagination of the space age.

FYInfo

The Space Race

Though rockets had been around on Earth since the thirteenth century in Asia, these rockets were generally used in warfare. It wasn't until the twentieth century that scientists considered using a rocket to explore space. Robert H. Goddard sent up the first liquid-fueled rocket in 1926. Then after World War II, some countries decided to build their own rockets to explore space. This was the beginning of the "space race" between the Soviet Union and the United States. The competition mirrored the political rivalries between the communist U.S.S.R. and the democratic U.S.

On October 4, 1957, the Soviet Union launched the first satellite, *Sputnik I*. The United States was quick to catch up, launching *Explorer I* on January 31, 1958. Then the Soviets and the Americans were in a race to see who could get the first human into space and eventually on the moon. In 1959, the Soviet lunar probe was the first to photograph the far side of the moon. In April 1961, Soviet cosmonaut Yuri Gagarin became the first person in space. One month later, U.S. President John F. Kennedy declared that the United States would send a man to the moon by the end of the decade.

All through the 1960s, people in NASA's Apollo program worked diligently on achieving Kennedy's dream. The program had a tragic setback when, during a test, the *Apollo 1* crew was killed in a cockpit fire. Subsequent

Yuri Gagarin's Space Capsule and Flight Suit

successful Apollo missions brought astronauts closer and closer to the moon. Finally, on July 20, 1969, *Apollo 11* landed on the moon, and Neil Armstrong became the first man to walk on the lunar surface. The Americans had achieved Kennedy's dream.

The United States and the Soviet Union continued to explore space, and in 1975 the two nations worked together on the Apollo-Soyuz Test Project, during which a U.S. spacecraft and Soviet spacecraft docked together in space. Since the fall of the Soviet Union in 1991, Russia and the United States have been working together on other space projects. Most notably, the two countries developed the International Space Station. The former competitors have been working as a team to explore the opportunities available in space.

On October 15, 2003, with the launch of *Shenzhou V,* China became the third nation to send a person into space.

In his Hollywood office, Ray Bradbury is surrounded by memorabilia from his books, films, and Disney projects. This photo was taken a few months after the debut of his long-running television show, *The Ray Bradbury Theater*.

Chapter 5

STILL WRITING

As might be expected of a writer with a dark side, Bradbury's favorite holiday is Halloween. He loves the mystery and history behind the holiday that he considers better than Christmas. After seeing the animated Peanuts Halloween special, *It's the Great Pumpkin, Charlie Brown,* Bradbury was inspired to create his own show. He wrote a script for a holiday special called *The Halloween Tree,* after a detailed picture he'd painted of a tree covered in jack-o'-lanterns. At first he was unable to sell the show, so he turned it into a story that was published as a book in 1972. In the book, a boy named Pip is kidnapped. In order to save him, his friends travel with a spirit called Mr. Moundshroud to the lands of Halloween past, where the children learn about customs related to Halloween. They see how other cultures, such as Mediterranean, Celtic, and Mexican, celebrate the holiday.

In addition to everything else that Bradbury was doing, his first book of poetry was published in 1973. Though he had been writing poetry as far back as high school, he didn't feel confident with this genre and waited many years to put his poems together in a book. The title of his collection—*When Elephants Last in the Dooryard Bloomed*—is a play on the title of Walt Whitman's poem "When Lilacs Last in the Dooryard Bloomed."

Around this time Bradbury began something that he had dreamed about for many years. He began consulting in architectural design. Inspired by rambling side streets of big cities, particularly those of Paris, Bradbury wanted to develop the same kind of feeling in urban malls. He wrote about his ideas, and it caught the attention of architect Jon Jerde. Bradbury was asked to help design several malls in Southern California, including the Glendale Galleria in the Los Angeles area and the Horton Plaza in San Diego. This was an incredible journey for the man who many years before had made cardboard buildings after going to the World's Fair in Chicago.

In the 1980s, some of Bradbury's works were shown on television. First, NBC made a miniseries based on *The Martian Chronicles*. Then in 1982, NBC adapted his story "I Sing the Body Electric," changing the title to *The Electric Grandmother*. The story is about a family who loses a mother and hires a robot to fill the role as a grandmother. During this time Bradbury also worked on turning *Something Wicked This Way Comes* into a movie. After a great deal of work and overcoming many obstacles, the film was released in 1983.

Soon Bradbury would have the opportunity to express his creativity a whole new way: he was getting his own television show. *The Ray Bradbury Theater* ran from 1985 until 1992. Bradbury wrote all of the episodes, and many big-name actors starred in the shows, including William Shatner, Tyne Daly, and Peter O'Toole. The series helped bring Ray's work to a whole new generation.

In 1985, Bradbury's first mystery novel, *Death Is a Lonely Business*, was published. In 1990 the sequel, *A Graveyard for Lunatics*, was released. Bradbury continued writing short stories as well, and in 1988, another short story collection, *The Toynbee Convector*, was published. In 1990 Bradbury put together a collection of essays on writing called *Zen in the Art of Writing*.

By this point Bradbury was considered a classic writer. Children in schools were reading his works along with other classic American writers such as William Faulkner, Emily Dickinson, and John Steinbeck. Another honor was bestowed on him in 1990. Waukegan, Illinois, dedicated Ray Bradbury Park to the man who wrote so fondly of his childhood home.

In 1998, another children's story, *Ahmed and the Oblivion Machines: A Fable,* was published. The story tells of a young boy who, after being lost in the desert, discovers an ancient god who teaches him how to fly.

In 1999, when Bradbury was at his vacation home in Palm Springs, California, he suffered a stroke. Hospitalized for a month and suffering from paralysis, he was determined to continue working. His daughter Alexandra sat beside him in the hospital to help him finish his last novel in his mystery trilogy, *Let's All Kill Constance.*

In the twenty-first century, Bradbury continues his contributions to literature. He still lives in his house in Los Angeles surrounded by toys and books. His favorite holiday is still Halloween, which he celebrates with enthusiasm every year. Bradbury explained, "I like the rawness, the nearness and the excitement of death, which went with the older vision of Halloween."[1] He also spoke of what he calls "October Country," where he finds "a year packed into a single month, a special climate which I still delight in. If I could have chosen my birthday, Halloween would be it."[2]

In November 2000, the National Book Foundation awarded Bradbury with the Medal for Distinguished Contribution to American Letters. He was thrilled to be so honored. In his acceptance speech, he said, "My dream always was that some day I could go to the library and look up on the shelf and see my own name gleaming against L. Frank Baum and the wonderful *Oz* books, or against Edgar Allan Poe's or leaning against many other similar writers and knowing that Jules Verne was on a shelf down below me along with H.G. Wells."[3]

In 2004, Bradbury traveled to Washington, D.C., where President George W. Bush awarded him the National Medal of Arts from The National Endowment for the Arts. The award states: "For his incomparable contributions to American fiction as one of its great storytellers who, through his explorations of science and space, has illuminated the human condition."[4]

Also that year, Bradbury made headlines when he denounced filmmaker Michael Moore for using the title *Fahrenheit 9/11* for his documentary movie on the policies of President George W. Bush and the war in the Middle East. He wasn't pleased that Moore had adapted his title, but Moore insisted it was too late to change it before the release of the film. The film was released as *Fahrenheit 9/11* as planned.

The new century brought other difficulties for Bradbury as well: he lost many people dear to him. In March 2001, he lost his aunt Neva, who had served as an inspiration to him as a child. In November 2003, Maggie died of lung cancer. She and Ray had been married fifty-six years. Then in April 2004, Ray lost his older brother, Skip.

Despite the deaths of those close to him and physical challenges from his stroke, Ray Bradbury continues to write and publish his works. In August 2005, his collection of essays, *Bradbury Speaks: Too Soon From the Cave, Too Far From the Stars,* was published. As he once stated in an interview, "Is writing easy for me? Yes, because it is a true joy. I am totally happy when I am plunged into the midst of adventures with my characters."[5] His writing has also brought joy to those who read his works.

Ray Bradbury changed the face of literature and has made his place with the classic writers he loves. He has also proved that through writing, one can "live forever."

FYInfo

Halloween

The pagan Celtic feast of Samhain celebrated the transition from fall to winter. It marked the time when the sun was halfway between the autumnal equinox (around September 22) and the winter solstice (December 21), the shortest day of the year in the northern hemisphere. The Celts believed that it was the one day of the year when the dead could return to the land of the living. Because of this belief, they also believed that evil spirits were especially powerful. They celebrated by burning fires and having ceremonies that reflected their fear and respect for the dead. By dressing up as someone dead, they believed that they could keep the dead from harming them. This is the origin of the tradition of dressing up as something scary on Halloween.

Later the Catholic Church turned the celebration into All Saints' Day and All Souls' Day (November first and second), which both honor the dead. The celebrations included fires, and the jack-o'-lanterns originated from an Irish story of a man named Jack who trapped the devil and made the devil promise to never take his soul. When Jack died, he was not allowed in heaven because of his stingy ways on Earth. He went down to hell, but the

devil would not take him because of the promise they had made. Instead, the devil gave Jack an ember from the fires of hell, which Jack placed in a turnip to light his way as he wandered the earth for eternity. Originally, jack-o'-lanterns were made from turnips or potatoes, and were lit to keep away the spirit of stingy Jack. When Irish people immigrated to the United States, they found that pumpkins were easier to obtain and carve.

In Britain groups of people called soulers would travel to houses and say a prayer for the dead in exchange for small cakes called soul cakes. Later, people would go house to house to gather "treats" without the prayers. This would become the modern practice of trick-or-treating.

CHRONOLOGY

1920   Rae Douglas Bradbury is born on August 22 in Waukegan, Illinois.

1923   Ray sees *The Hunchback of Notre Dame* with his mother, sparking his love of films.

1926   Ray's sister Elizabeth is born. The Bradbury family moves to Tucson, Arizona.

1927   The family moves back to Waukegan.

1928   Elizabeth dies.

1929   Ray discovers *Buck Rogers of the 25th Century*.

1932   The Bradbury family moves back to Tucson, Arizona.

1933   The family returns to Waukegan; Ray attends the World's Fair in Chicago.

1934   The Bradbury family moves to Los Angeles, California.

1938   Ray graduates from Los Angeles High School. His first published short story appears in *Imagination!*

1942   Bradbury writes "The Lake."

1947   Ray and Maggie are married.

1949   Bradbury's first daughter, Susan, is born.

1951   Bradbury's second daughter, Ramona, is born.

1953   Bradbury and his family go to Ireland, where Ray works on the screenplay for *Moby Dick* for John Huston.

1955   Bradbury's third daughter, Bettina, is born.

1957   Bradbury's father dies.

1958   Bradbury's fourth daughter, Alexandra, is born.

1964   The World's Fair includes Bradbury's *American Journey* exhibit. Bradbury meets Walt Disney.

1966   Bradbury's mother dies.

1967   Bradbury meets the *Apollo 1* astronauts

1982   The Epcot Center opens in Disney World, with Bradbury's *Spaceship Earth* exhibit.

1983   The film version of *Something Wicked This Way Comes* is released.

1999   Bradbury suffers a stroke.

2000   He is awarded the National Book Foundation's Medal for Distinguished Contribution to American Letters.

2003   Maggie Bradbury dies from lung cancer.

2004   Ray Bradbury is awarded the National Medal of Arts from The National Endowment for the Arts.

2005   Bradbury receives the Mars Exploration Award from the Planetary Society.

2006   Discussions are under way for Ray Bradbury to adapt his story "Dark They Were, And Golden-Eyed" for the ABC series *Master's of Science Fiction*.

SELECTED WORKS

TIMELINE IN HISTORY

1867   Christopher Scholes invents the modern typewriter.

1877   Edweard Muybridge invents the first moving pictures.

1884   L. N. Thompson opens the first roller coaster in Coney Island.

1901   The first transatlantic radio signal is transmitted.

1906   Kellogg's starts selling a new cereal, cornflakes.

1918   Influenza pandemic sweeps the globe and kills millions.

1920   Women are given the right to vote in the United States.

1928   *Steamboat Willie,* Walt Disney's first Mickey Mouse cartoon with synchronized sound, is shown.

1930   Pluto, the ninth planet in the solar system, is discovered.

1938   Orson Welles' radio broadcast of *The War of the Worlds* on Halloween causes some to believe that the U.S. is under attack by Martians.

1941   The Japanese attack Pearl Harbor and the U.S. enters World War II.

1945   The first atomic bomb is detonated, effectively ending the war.

1950   Senator Joseph McCarthy begins his communist scare.

1957   The Soviet Union launches *Sputnik I* into orbit.

1958   NASA is created.

1962   John Glenn becomes the first American to orbit Earth.

1963   U.S. President John F. Kennedy is assassinated.

1966   The *Star Trek* television series begins.

1977   The movie *Star Wars* is released.

1983   Sally Ride becomes the first American woman in space.

1990   Hubble Space Telescope launched.

1996   Scientists successfully clone sheep.

2003   With the launch of *Shenzhou V,* China becomes the third country to send an astronaut into space.

2004   American Mike Melvill flies the first privately funded spacecraft, *SpaceShipOne,* out of Earth's atmosphere.

2005   NASA's Deep Impact probe successfully strikes and scatters debris from a comet.

2006   NASA's Stardust spacecraft successfully brings comet particles to Earth for scientific study.

CHAPTER NOTES

Chapter One
A Life of Imagination

1. Sam Weller, *The Bradbury Chronicles* (New York: William Morrow, 2005), p. 303.

Chapter Two
Films, Books, and Comic Strips

1. Steven L. Aggelis, editor, *Conversations with Ray Bradbury* (Jackson, Miss.: University Press of Mississippi, 2004), p. 86.

2. Ibid., p. 20.

3. Ray Bradbury, "In His Words," http://www.raybradbury.com/inhiswords02.html

4. Ibid.

5. Aggelis, p. 163.

6. Sam Weller, *The Bradbury Chronicles* (New York: William Morrow, 2005), p. 113.

Chapter Three
The Journey to Success

1. Steven L. Aggelis, editor, *Conversations with Ray Bradbury* (Jackson, Miss.: University Press of Mississippi, 2004), p. 90.

2. Ibid., p. 139.

3. Ibid., p. 99.

4. Ibid., p. 19.

5. Ibid., p. 22.

6. Ibid., pp. 52–53.

Chapter Four
The Moon and Beyond

1. Andrew Chaikin, *A Man on the Moon* (New York: Penguin Books, 1995), p. 15.

2. Steven L. Aggelis, editor, *Conversations with Ray Bradbury* (Jackson, Miss.: University Press of Mississippi, 2004), pp. 126–127.

Chapter Five
Still Writing

1. Steven L. Aggelis, editor, *Conversations with Ray Bradbury* (Jackson, Miss.: University Press of Mississippi, 2004), p. 36.

2. Ibid., p. 20.

3. Ray Bradbury, "National Book Award Acceptance Speech," http://www.nationalbook.org/nbaacceptspeech_rbradbury.html

4. National Endowment for the Arts, "2004 National Medal of Arts: Ray Bradbury," http://www.nea.gov/news/news04/medals/Bradbury.html

5. Aggelis, p. 25.

FURTHER READING

For Young Adults

Bradbury, Ray. *The Best of Ray Bradbury: The Graphic Novel*. New York and London: Simon & Schuster, 2003.

Kelly, Nigel. *The Moon Landing: The Race into Space*. Oxford: Heinemann Library, 2001.

Lackmann, Ron. *Comic Strips and Comic Books of Radio's Golden Age, 1920s–1950s*. Boalsburg, Penn.: BearManor Media, 2004.

Silverberg, Robert, editor. *The Science Fiction Hall of Fame: Volume One, 1929–1964*. New York: Tor Books, 2003.

Works Consulted

Aggelis, Steven L., editor. *Conversations with Ray Bradbury*. Jackson: University Press of Mississippi, 2004.

Asimov, Isaac. *Library of the Universe: Mars*. Milwaukee: Gareth Stevens Publishers, 1994.

———. *Library of the Universe: Rockets, Probes, and Satellites*. Milwaukee: Gareth Stevens Publishers, 1988.

Chaikin, Andrew. *A Man on the Moon*. New York: Penguin Books, 1995.

Cleere, Gail S. "Halfway to Winter." *Natural History*. October 1992.

Halberstam, David. *The Fifties*. New York: Villard Books, 1993.

Weller, Sam. *The Bradbury Chronicles*. New York: William Morrow, 2005.

On the Internet

Blanding, Michael. "A Brief History of Carnivals." *Pacific News Service*.
http://www.pacificnews.org/jinn/stories/3.17/970814-carnival.html

Bradbury, Ray.
http://www.raybradbury.com

Buck Rogers.
http://www.buck-rogers.com/

Jet Propulsion Laboratory. *Mars Exploration Rovers*.
http://www.jpl.nasa.gov/missions/mer/

NASA. *The Apollo Program*.
http://nssdc.gsfc.nasa.gov/planetary/lunar/apollo.html

GLOSSARY

**anthology
(an-THAH-luh-jee)**
A collection of related literary works.

**Apollo
(ah-PAH-loe)**
The Greek god of the sun. NASA adopted the name for the space program designed to send a human to the moon.

**chronicle
(KRAH-nih-kul)**
A detailed account of events.

Cold War
The period of nonviolent animosity between the United States and the Soviet Union in the late twentieth century.

**communist
(KAH-myoo-nist)**
A political system in which there is no private industry; instead, companies are controlled by the government.

**endowment
(en-DOW-mint)**
Funds or property given to an individual or group; also, a natural ability or gift.

**Fahrenheit
(FAA-ren-hite)**
A temperature scale that measures the freezing point of water at 32 degrees and the boiling point at 212 degrees.

**genre
(JHAN-ra)**
A category of music or literature marked by a distinctive style, form, or content.

**pseudonym
(SUE-duh-nim)**
A fictitious name, especially a pen name.

INDEX